EASTER
SEASON OF PASSION

WORSHIP THROUGH THE SEASONS

DAVID M. EDWARDS

B&H
PUBLISHING GROUP
NASHVILLE, TENNESSEE

Advent: Season of Passion
Worship Through the Seasons Series
Copyright © 2007 by David M. Edwards
All Rights Reserved

ISBN 0-8054-4332-0
ISBN-13: 978-0-8054-4332-5
B&H Publishing Group
Nashville, Tennessee
www.BHPublishingGroup.com

Dewey Decimal Classification: 242
Devotional Literature \ Worship

Printed in China
1 2 3 4 09 08 07 06

To Glenda

Thank you for understanding and championing my Passion.

With deep gratitude,

David

Creation groaned; the earth did grieve
When God's own Son hung on a Tree,
Willingly His life for us
'Twas bound only once

Never could they hold Him down,
No defeat for love's dear Crown,
Greater glory ne'er displayed
By the Author of this grace

What Deity would leave His throne
To search the earth for only one,
Gather up our filthy flesh
And crown it in His righteousness

Bound only once to set me free,
Tears and blood poured down for me,
Precious Saviour, wounded Priest,
'Twas bound only once.

—David M. Edwards and Margaret Becker

This is one of four books in a devotional series called **Worship Through the Seasons.** These seasonal books mirror the calendar year: Advent, Easter, Pentecost, Harvest. Rather than using a daily devotional template, I wanted to offer writings that would coincide with a particular time of the year and could be read and contemplated throughout that season. My hope is to make the year meaningful as you discover topics and Scriptures themed for each season.

Season of Passion represents **Easter**—that painful, horrific, yet death-defying season when the Good Shepherd laid down His life for His sheep and rose again from the dead! What Jesus willingly did for us still brings tears to our eyes and causes us to tremble. God's all-encompassing love was poured out on a Cross one dark afternoon in Jerusalem so long ago. This set of devotional writings centers around the passion of Jesus Christ and the price paid for our pardon. May these words lead you to a place of worship where you can come to know His sufferings and yet stand in the glow and power of a vacant tomb! Walk with me through God's **Season of Passion**.

He was despised and rejected by men, a man of suffering who knew what sickness was. He was like one people turned away from; He was despised, and we didn't value Him. Yet He Himself bore our sicknesses, and He carried our pains; but we in turn regarded Him stricken, struck down by God, and afflicted.

But He was pierced because of our transgressions, crushed because of our iniquities; punishment for our peace was on Him, and we are healed by His wounds. We all went astray like sheep; we all have turned to our own way; and the Lord has punished Him for the iniquity of us all.

Isaiah 53:3–7

CHAPTER 1

JESUS, THE TRUE SHEPHERD

WORDS OF PASSION FROM JOHN 10

ONE OF THE MOST BEAUTIFUL PICTURES OF our Savior is the Bible's depiction of Him as our Shepherd. It is an image rich in both history and humility, in age and affection. Safe and reassuring. Strong. Stable. Loving.

Shepherd.

The conspicuous number of shepherds in Old Testament days, from Abel on down, prepared Israel for the manifestation of the Messiah as their True Shepherd, a personal shepherd. God had even revealed Himself to them by the name *Jehovah-Rohi*—"The Lord Your Shepherd."

"Shepherd" in the Hebrew language had several meanings to the children of Israel: feeder, keeper, companion, friend, pastor, herdsman, shepherd. Truly, the Lord is our Feeder to provide, Keeper to protect, Companion to cheer, Friend to help, Pastor to comfort, Herdsman to gather, Shepherd to lead. How rich with both spiritual and practical significance is this title of our Lord—"Shepherd."

When it comes to the Greek word for "shepherd" used in the New Testament, we see that the shepherd is a herdsman, one who tends, leads, guides, cherishes, feeds, and protects a flock. The New Testament uses this word to describe a Christian pastor who faithfully leads those who are entrusted to his care (Ephesians 4:11). The term is also applied metaphorically to Christ, both in His own words and in the words of the Epistles (John 10:11; 14, 16; Hebrews 13:20; 1 Peter 2:25).

To those of us living on this side of the Cross, we can certainly attest to the validity that Jesus Christ is in fact our True Shepherd. He daily leads us and provides for us. This single title alone—Shepherd—conjures up feelings and mental pictures of safety, comfort, and care.

It's why the Twenty-third Psalm is standard fare throughout the world for times of crises and tragedy. Our Shepherd Messiah brings a peace and comfort to us that this world cannot offer.

OLD TESTAMENT FORESHADOWINGS

Along the path to their destiny and throughout their early history, God frequently revealed Himself to His chosen people as their *Jehovah-Rohi*, the One whose love, care, and resources they could depend upon in all the untrodden and unknown pathways of the future. No matter what their unseen days ahead might produce, whether temporal or spiritual, their faithful Shepherd would be there at every turn to relieve and undertake.

The children of Israel saw mirrors of themselves in the faces of defenseless sheep and lambs, which require someone stronger than themselves to guard them from adversaries and their own natural frailties. Human instinct and intuition told them that they could not live as sheep without a shepherd. The Lord God Almighty was the One they needed to feed them as His flock, gather them within His arms, and carry them in His bosom.

This figure of the shepherd was used repeatedly in the Old Testament to illustrate the close relationship between a leader and his people. Second Samuel records the tribes of Israel saying this to David: "Even while Saul was king over us, you were the one who led us out to battle and brought us back. The Lord also said to you, 'You will shepherd My people Israel and be ruler over Israel'" (2 Samuel 5:2).

It is in the phrase "the Lord is my Shepherd," however, that this relationship between leader and people finds its highest and most tender expression. Yes, Jehovah is awful and unapproachable in His unrivaled holiness, as Moses realized (Exodus 33:20). But as Shepherd, He comes near to touch, shield, defend, and—yes!—even lay down His life for us!

NEW TESTAMENT FULFILLMENT

Recognizing that the Old Testament is full of types and shadows of things to come, we see in Jesus the New Testament fulfillment of the shepherd's role. Truly, no title of God is more beautifully pictured and personified in Christ than that of *Jehovah-Rohi*—"The Lord Your Shepherd"—whose wondrous birth was first announced to shepherds tending their flocks on a hillside outside Bethlehem. They were witnesses to the advent of the True and Good Shepherd who came to seek and save that which was lost. I can just imagine that Jesus' own disciples must have loved this image of Him as their Shepherd, for they had seen and experienced firsthand His tender care and mercy. They observed His shepherd heart melt with compassion over the multitudes that came to Him having no shepherd. They experienced the power of the Shepherd's call when He commanded Lazarus to awaken from death. They heard and believed the

> **HE WILL TEND THEM HIMSELF AND WILL BE THEIR SHEPHERD.**
> **(EZEKIEL 34:23)**

Shepherd's promise to carry them between His shoulders until they were safely home. More than all of this, they saw the depth of a Shepherd's love for His sheep, poured out in blood on a cruel Cross! Jesus was their Shepherd every step of the way.

THE RELATIONSHIP BETWEEN SHEPHERD AND SHEEP

As the True Shepherd, Jesus comes near to us even now to touch us, love us, and protect us. Jesus has come that all who receive Him may have life in its fullest sense—the eternal life of the kingdom of God. The death of the Shepherd embraces all people.

Jesus said again, "I assure you: I am the door of the sheep. All who came before me are thieves and robbers, but the sheep didn't listen to them. I am the door. If anyone enters by Me, he will be saved and will come in and go out and find pasture. A thief comes only to steal and to kill and to destroy. I have come that they may have life and have it in abundance.

I am the good shepherd. The good shepherd lays down his life for the sheep. . . . I am the good shepherd. I know My own sheep, and they know Me, as the Father knows Me, and I know the Father. I lay down My life for the sheep."

John 10:7–11, 14–15

To the Greeks, knowledge was synonymous with seeing. Only by seeing something did they think they could comprehend its nature. The Hebrews, however, believed that true knowledge was synonymous with experience. To truly know about something meant to have a relationship with that something. This is very important for us to understand as we look at this passage from

John 10, because even though the New Testament was written in Greek, its writers (and the apostles) were Hebrew. Thus, when Jesus spoke of knowing His sheep and being known by them, they knew that "knowing" meant more than having a head knowledge of who He was. It meant a relationship, an experience, walking with Him day by day, week by week, year by year.

The relationship between our Shepherd and us—between Jesus Christ and His flock—is grounded in the nature of the relationship between Jesus and the Father: "I am the good shepherd. I *know* My own sheep, and they *know* Me, as the Father *knows* Me, and I *know* the Father" (John 10:14–15). When Jesus used the word "know," He was saying that His sheep know Him by experience. We know Him through having actual contact with Him. We have a history with Jesus as our Shepherd, which produces a common bond of deep love and fidelity.

The disciples' relationship with Jesus as their Shepherd was tested to its limits during the days of His arrest and crucifixion. Would they still believe in Him? Would they still believe He was their Messiah? Would they stand by His side until the very end?

Or would they once again be sheep without a shepherd? Jesus predicted what would happen on the eve of the Last Supper:

> Then Jesus said to them, "Tonight all of you will run away because of Me, for it is written: 'I will strike the shepherd, and the sheep will be scattered.'"
>
> Matthew 26:31

OUR FATHERS TRUSTED IN YOU; THEY TRUSTED, AND YOU RESCUED THEM. (PSALM 22:4)

"Strike the Shepherd, and the sheep will be scattered." This is a tragic principle illustrated time and again throughout church history. Without a shepherd, sheep will scatter in every direction. Quite naturally, then, when the Voice the disciples had heard every day for three years fell suddenly silent, they had trouble believing that what was about to take place was ordained by Father God, that Jesus was simply submitting to His Father's will.

Jesus had told them before, "I lay down My life for the sheep."

Now came the fulfillment of what He had promised—to put into effect a New Covenant in which all who believed in Him could receive forgiveness of sins and fellowship with God.

The Shepherd was doing what shepherds do. But what about the sheep? What would their response be to this singular act of sacrificial devotion?

OUR BLEEDING SHEPHERD

In John 19, we see and read the unthinkable. It tells us of a love without limit that refused to back away or cower in fear. Instead He boldly, bravely, and graciously paid sin's price for each of us. The whole purpose of Jesus' mission was to impart life—a life supreme in quality as well as infinite and eternal in quantity. God's purpose and plan were not only to save man from death, destruction, and guilt, but also to make him holy, "conformed to the image of His Son" (Romans 8:29). Such purpose could be achieved in only one way—the voluntary death of Jesus.

The death of the Shepherd.

When Jesus aligned Himself with the will of the Father, resurrection was made possible and actual. He gave the Father something to resurrect, something to vindicate. A holy Shepherd's body and blood purchased freedom for everyone wanting to be a part of His eternal flock. Through the gift of Himself, He provided everlasting life for each one of His lambs.

And now our entire lives can be fixed upon faith in our true and lasting Shepherd who was obedient to His Father's will. Jesus' sacrificial death on the Cross was the apex of His entire life and ministry. *It is what He came to do!* The True Shepherd came to lay down His life—once and for all—for His sheep!

THE VOICE OF THE BLEEDING SHEPHERD

It's easy to hear His voice when He calls us to green pastures and to graze beside still waters. It's easy to hear His voice when He calls us to great blessing and to times of great joy. But can we hear the voice that calls us to sacrifice?

Can we hear the voice that calls us from our comfort zones to a place where He can stretch and expand us for His purposes and plans? Can we hear His voice saying, "Could you not stay awake with Me one hour?" (Matt. 26:40). Can we hear His voice as He calls us to intercede in the garden? Can we hear His voice calling us to crucifixion, laying down our lives in obedience to Him and for the sake of others?

Jesus will always call us to a Gethsemane where we must say, "Not my will, but Yours be done." Jesus will always call us to sacrifice, to lay on the altar our carnal way of doing things and our selfish thoughts and plans. Jesus, our Bleeding Shepherd, calls us to lay our lives down in loving submission to Him so that He can raise us up to be the men and women of God that He has called us to be.

His sheep know His voice. They follow where He leads. And today His voice is calling us to follow His example of selfless living and loving sacrifice, preferring others above ourselves, refusing to sin, refusing to retaliate, refusing to manipulate others, refusing to act defensively, bearing the burdens and sins of others so that they might receive healing and reconciliation.

This is what He calls us to.

It's not always easy, but His way is always best. Our personal wholeness flows out of our encounter with the Bleeding Shepherd of Calvary. And the more closely we follow and heed His call, the more complete and whole we become.

> For you were called to this, because Christ also suffered for you, leaving you an example, so that you should follow in His steps. He "did not commit sin, and no deceit was found in His mouth"; when reviled, He did not revile in return; when suffering, He did not threaten, but committed Himself to the One who judges justly. He himself bore our sins in His body on the tree, so that, having died to sins, we might live for righteousness; by "His wounding you have been healed." For you "were like sheep going astray," but you have now returned to the shepherd and guardian of your souls.
>
> *1 Peter 2:21-25*

This is what we are called to. His life is our example, our pattern to follow. Our Shepherd is calling and we must follow. No matter where He leads, follow on!

Let us continually pray throughout this Easter season, "Lord, may my life be an imprint of who You are! I will follow Your voice even when the way seems dark, for I trust in Your love for me. You will always be by my side leading me into victory, triumph, and glory. Should I fall or become weary, You will carry me until I am able to walk again. May I ever keep my cross nearby, for my life is in your hands. I worship and praise You, my True Shepherd."

In Jesus' Name, amen.

THE CHARACTERISTIC FEATURE OF A GOOD shepherd is his willingness to give his very life for his sheep. Jesus, of course, applied this level of sacrifice to Himself, saying, "I lay down My life for the sheep" (John 10:11, 15).

"Sheep" refers not only to those who received Him as Messiah in the days of His earthly life, the ones who actually heard His human voice calling them "My sheep," but to an entire world full of sinners lost and ruined by the Fall—sheep who have gone astray (Isaiah 53:6). It applies to us. All of our iniquity was laid upon Jesus who, as our Good Shepherd, bared His breast to receive the sword of judgment (Zechariah 13:7).

We will never know all that was involved in the laying down of His life. We will never grasp what was required for us to be counted among those sheep that bear the blood-mark of the Good Shepherd. None of the ransomed and redeemed will ever know what Jesus had to pass through in order to make it possible for Him to go after each and every lost little lamb. "Yet it pleased the Lord to bruise Him; He has put Him to grief" (Isaiah 53:10, NKJV). It was the Father's plan to bruise or crush the sin offering for our redemption. Knowing that, Jesus willingly submitted to the Father's will. He made Himself an offering for our sins. Christ, the Good Shepherd, was the only one good enough to die as the Lamb of God.

Jesus would not have been crucified had He not resigned Himself to the fact and submitted to His Father's will. In this, we see His goodness. Our Good Shepherd became the good sacrifice, making it possible for His Goodness to dwell in our hearts by His Holy Spirit!

The word "good" in the Greek is a descriptive word signifying that which is noble, beautiful, pleasing, acceptable, excellent, serviceable, attractive, and honest. Sure sounds like Jesus, doesn't it! Everything about Him is good. Everything He's about is good. He isn't just good—He is Goodness!

THE DOOR OF THE SHEEP

Jesus declared Himself the "door of the sheep" in verses 7 and 9 from John 10. In other words, there's only one way to salvation, only one way of receiving eternal life, only one way to peace, provision, and abundant living—only one way! And that way passes through the door named Jesus! No man can get to God except through Jesus Christ His Son.

> *Jesus told them, "I am the way, the truth, and the life.*
> *No one comes to the Father except through Me."*
> *John 14:6*

Whenever you hear someone talk about, announce, or proclaim the gift of life apart from salvation by faith in Jesus Christ, they are in actuality proclaiming themselves to be thieves and robbers, securing for themselves a future in hell for their destructive activity.

That's because it's not enough to be a morally good person. You must be born again!

Most assuredly, I am saying to you, He who does not go through the door into the walled-in enclosure for the sheep, but climbs up from some other quarter, that one is a thief and a robber. But he who enters through the door is a shepherd of the sheep. To this one the doorkeeper opens. And the sheep hear his voice, and he personally calls the sheep which are his private possession by name and leads them out. Whenever he puts forth all who are his very own, before them he proceeds, and the sheep follow with him because they know his voice. But one belonging to another flock they will positively not follow, but will run away from him because they do not know the voice of the others.
John 10:1–5 (An Expanded Translation)

Many claim to be shepherds but are powerless to save. There's only one Good Shepherd. There's only one Savior. Be careful in putting people up on pedestals. It's all right to admire people, to revere those whom God uses in your life. But always remember that they had to be saved just like you. *They are not your savior!* They did not die for you—and even if they could, it would be useless. Jesus alone is our salvation! Follow people who are following Jesus and in love with Him, people who brag on Jesus and not on themselves.

The "door of the sheep" is a symbol of the entrant's legitimacy, the proof of the Shepherd's right to receive us as His own. By its very nature, this "door" rules out all other claimants to being saviors of humankind. Jesus alone is the door to salvation and

> **TURN TO ME AND BE SAVED, ALL THE ENDS OF THE EARTH. (ISAIAH 45:22)**

safekeeping. All others are false gods. Jesus is the only way in.

So when Jesus speaks of "thieves and robbers," He is warning us to beware of those who seek to draw us away from our Shepherd, those who use the same argument as the Pharisees, saying in essence, "Follow me, because I do what the Bible really says." There are even people who will say, "Don't listen to your Christian friend. Listen to me. I know what God is really saying." Thieves and robbers will always point you to another way in. Don't listen to them!

The only way in is through the Door, and the Door is Jesus!

> *I am the good shepherd. The good shepherd lays down his life for the sheep. The hired man, since he is not the shepherd and doesn't own the sheep, leaves them and runs away when he sees a wolf coming. The wolf then snatches and scatters them. This happens because he is a hired man and doesn't care about the sheep.*
>
> *John 10:11–13*

Besides "thieves and robbers," Jesus also warns against "hired" men. A hired man is a "wage-earner." His sense of responsibility lies in what he can get rather than what he can give.

Jesus made it perfectly clear that one does not have to be a thief, robber, or wolf to destroy the sheep. A mere wage-earner is dangerous enough. And believe me, they're much harder to spot—and much easier to become! Unless we keep a close guard on our motives, keeping our hearts pure in serving others, we'll be overwhelmed when the wolves of crises come. We will flee and forsake our responsibilities in the kingdom and our responsibility to the flock.

You can see people's true loyalties when you ask them to give for a particular need or to serve for a worthy cause. The hired hands will always turn you down! They'll always have something else to do, an excuse for why they can't help out or why they didn't show up. They have no sense of responsibility to the flock of God.

Hired hands in the kingdom of God get out of the way at the first sign of trouble, because they're only in it for themselves. Jesus says to watch out for these kinds of people, those who are more concerned about what they get out of God or can get out of the Church rather than what they can give or can do to help, defend, and protect her.

Jesus our Good Shepherd says to us today, "I am the door. All who enter through me will be saved. All who enter through me will find abundant eternal life. All who enter through me will have all that they need in order to be delivered from sin, guilt, and condemnation. I am the door and none other exists!"

This Jesus is "the stone despised by you builders, who has become the cornerstone." There is salvation in no one else, for there is no other name under heaven given to people by which we must be saved.

Acts 4:11–12

OVER MY DEAD BODY

Still today in the Middle East, shepherds set up corrals to be used in the evening when it's time for the flocks to be gathered in. The shepherds speak of themselves as a "door of the sheep," because they lie down across the open entry of the sheepfold, and their body forms a barrier or door to any intruder, whether thieves or wild beasts. They lay down their very lives between the sheep and the rest of the world. What a clear and vivid picture this paints for us. Jesus, the Good Shepherd, lying down across the entrance to the pastures of the Lord, where any thief, robber,

> I WILL SAY:
> THEY ARE MY PEOPLE,
> AND THEY WILL SAY:
> THE LORD IS OUR GOD.
> (ZECHARIAH 13:9)

wolf, or wild beast would have to step over the Shepherd in order to get to His sheep.

Even while we sheep are bedded down for the night, our Shepherd uses His own body to protect us as we sleep. All looks fine in the morning light, but the Shepherd alone knows how many enemies He had to fend off during the night so that we could be secure and at peace.

Jesus is our Good Shepherd. He is the Door. No one can come in without first going through Him.

UNDERSTANDING HIS VOICE

In ancient Judea, three or four shepherds would gather together at one of the many wells dotting the countryside. While they relaxed and talked with others, their individual flocks would begin to mingle together. Thus, the three or four separate flocks would become one big flock of sheep, all mixed together. When it was time for the shepherds to go, however, the men didn't go through all the sheep and pick out which ones were theirs. They didn't have to spend all day long separating the sheep. The sheep would naturally divide themselves back into the three or four flocks from which they had originally come by following the distinctive call of their own shepherd. Even amid the calling of three, four, or more voices, each sheep could discern which voice to follow, which voice was familiar, which voice brought them comfort and made them feel safe.

Sheep know the voice of their shepherd.

> *I am the good shepherd. I know My own sheep, and they know Me, as the Father knows Me, and I know the Father. I lay down My life for the sheep. But I have other sheep that are not of this fold; I must bring them also, and they will listen to My voice. Then there will be one flock, one shepherd.*
>
> *John 10:14–16*

Can you hear His voice today? He calls you to His fold, and the only way in is through the Door. Once inside, He will give you abundant life forever, providing for your every need. There's not an enemy in hell that can intrude without His knowing it and without His defeating it.

In life we will encounter pretend shepherds offering cheap, low-quality care, strange voices that bid us to come and follow down every path imaginable. But let us not be fooled! We know the voice of the One who loves us and has laid down His life for us.

Even as the shepherd lies across the opening to the fold, becoming the door for his sheep on a daily basis, I believe that Jesus—our Good Shepherd—loves us so much that He would die for us again and again!

CHAPTER 3

MORE THAN ANY OTHER BOOK IN THE NEW Testament, Hebrews bridges the gap between the Old Testament's covenantal worship systems—presented as types and shadows of things to come—and their fulfillment in the person and work of Jesus, the Messiah.

The writer of Hebrews eloquently explains how Jesus became the embodiment of everything we hope for and need in a Savior. It is in these sacred ancient words that we find again the beloved picture of a shepherd, and find yet another title due Him—the Great Shepherd of the sheep!

Jesus has come so that all in the world may have life in its fullest sense—the eternal life of the kingdom of God. The death of the Shepherd embraces all people, and the resurrection of the Shepherd makes His embrace eternal to those who will follow Him.

*Now may the God of peace who brought up from the
dead our Lord Jesus—the great Shepherd of the
sheep—with the blood of the everlasting covenant,
equip you with all that is good to do His will, working in
us what is pleasing in His sight, through Jesus Christ,
to whom be glory forever and ever. Amen.*

Hebrews 13:20–21

Had Jesus remained dead, He would not have been able to function as our Great Shepherd. But praise be to God, Jesus Himself declared: "Don't be afraid! I am the First and the Last, and the Living One. I was dead, but look—I am alive forever and ever, and I hold the keys of death and Hades" (Revelation 1:17–18).

The writer of Hebrews indicates that while the Shepherd was good because He was willing to die for the lost that they might be the sheep in His eternal fold, He became the Great Shepherd because He rose again! Look again at those verses:

*Now the God of peace, the One who brought up out
from among the dead the Shepherd of the sheep, the*

Great One, in the blood of an eternal testament, our Lord Jesus, equip you in every good thing to do His will, doing that in you which is well pleasing in His sight through Jesus Christ, to whom be the glory forever and ever. Amen.

Hebrews 13:20–21 (An Expanded Translation)

Herbert Lockyer writes, "The God of Peace, Jehovah-Shalom, brought forth Jesus Christ out from among the dead. Now as the Living Christ, He cares for His own, making them to lie down in pastures of green, and leading them beside the quiet waters of refreshment. He knows our every need, and as all power is His, He can and does care for us as the Greatest Shepherd ever."[1]

Now He can make us complete and present us before the Father without fault. His covenant is eternal and will be in effect forever.

BROUGHT BACK FROM THE DEAD

Before God brought His people "up out from among the dead," He brought them up out of the land of Egypt:

Then he remembered the days of old,
Moses and his people, saying:
"Where is He who brought them up out of the sea
With the shepherd of His flock?
Where is He who put His Holy Spirit within them,
Who led them by the right hand of Moses,
With His glorious arm,
Dividing the water before them
To make for Himself an everlasting name,
Who led them through the deep,
As a horse in the wilderness,
That they might not stumble?"
As a beast goes down into the valley,
And the Spirit of the Lord causes him to rest,
So You lead Your people,
To make Yourself a glorious name.

Isaiah 63:11–14

This Old Testament passage refers to God's appointment of Moses as the leader of Israel in the context of the deliverance from Egypt. Moses, the shepherd of Midian (Exodus 3:1), was the model for the Great Shepherd, Jesus. According to these verses, Moses was led forth and brought out not as an isolated individual but as the shepherd of the flock. The entire people are specified as the object of God's leading.

This is true of Jesus, as well, who was led forth from the realm of the dead. Through Him God has begun to lead His flock in order to make a glorious name for Himself, an action that will be complete when the entire flock of God is brought to an experience of celebrative rest in His eternal glory and presence.

> HE DIED TO SIN ONCE FOR ALL; BUT IN THAT HE LIVES, HE LIVES TO GOD. (ROMANS 6:10)

This is Christ's role as our Great Shepherd. It is the reason why He was appointed to this high office. You and I were and are the objects of God's leading Jesus out from among the dead. In order for us to be brought safely into His fold, He had to bring Jesus up out from among the dead first! Jesus became the "firstfruits" from among the dead—guaranteeing more to come!

> *But now Christ has been raised from the dead, the firstfruits of those who have fallen asleep. For since death came through a man, the resurrection of the dead also comes through a man. For just as in Adam all die, so also in Christ all will be made alive. But each in his own order: Christ, the firstfruits; afterward, at His coming, the people of Christ.*
>
> *1 Corinthians 15:20–23*

The resurrection of Jesus Christ demonstrates God's decisive intervention by which He acknowledged and ratified the Cross of Christ as the means of redemption for the human family.

In the Isaiah passage, God's instructions to Moses were to lead the people out from the sea and into the Promised Land. In the Hebrews passage, God's will was for Jesus to lead us and bring us out of the realm of the dead. Jesus paved the way out of death and hell for you and me. He led the way!

This "bringing out" is the fundamental redemptive action of God under both the old and new covenants. Upon it are based the exclusive claims of God to His people's allegiance, as well as the ground for our trust in His power and readiness to stand by us, His covenant people. The intervention of God in leading His people out of Egypt prefigured His decisive action in raising Jesus from the dead. Yet again, we have another "type and shadow" fulfilled in the coming and ministry of Christ.

Therefore, God has established a new covenant with His people through the "bringing out" of Jesus from the realm of the dead. This is the fundamental action of God that has replaced the foundational acts of salvation under the Old Covenant. Although Moses was "the shepherd of the sheep" whom God "brought out" from the land of Egypt, Jesus is "the great shepherd of the sheep" whom God "brought out" from the realm of the dead. Jesus alone is the Mediator—the go-between—of an everlasting covenant.

"BROUGHT" BY THE BLOOD

This phrase in Hebrews 13:20—"with the blood of the everlasting covenant"—is better understood this way: "*because of* the blood of the everlasting covenant" or "*by virtue of* the blood of the everlasting covenant." Jesus Christ was led out from among the dead by virtue of the unique and unrepeatable pouring out of His own blood (Hebrews 9:18–28; 10:11–18).

He died on the cross as a covenant sacrifice. He then entered into the heavenly sanctuary and sprinkled His own blood as an offering to pay for our sins. The resurrection of Jesus Christ occurred by virtue of the sprinkling of His blood in the heavenly sanctuary and the establishment of the new covenant.

We must understand that the obtaining of the blood and the sprinkling of the blood belong indissolubly together. His body and blood being offered in the heavenly sanctuary are associated yet successive actions. Good Friday is the great Day of Atonement for the human family with God, for those who trust in His saving grace through faith. The blood of the covenant effects the sanctification of the new covenant people. We are "bought" by the blood because He "brought" the blood.

Indeed, Jesus' work and sacrifice are the basis for the everlasting covenant. Without them, there would be no Easter—no "everlasting" or "eternal covenant," no future event that will bring with it an enduring closeness to God. Without the sacrifice of Jesus, there is no "new covenant in My blood," no replacing of the Old Covenant. Even greater, the gift of the New Covenant is not provisional or temporary. It is God's final, costly forgiveness, which in no way glosses over or condones our sin but is altogether worthy of God, who in all His ways is holy, righteous, and true.

Through His blood the exalted Jesus once and for all time accomplished the atonement for the people of God and established an eternal covenant. "IT IS FINISHED!" he cried from the Cross. Now we can come boldly to the Throne of Grace, no longer cut off but brought near by His blood. You and I belong to the fold of "the great Shepherd" because we have been sealed by an everlasting blood covenant and by the precious deposit of His Holy Spirit.

Because Jesus came up and out of the realm of the dead, *we will too!*—following our Great Shepherd forever!

[1]Lockyer, Herbert. *All the Divine Names and Titles in the Bible* (Grand Rapids: Zondervan, 1975), 50.

CHAPTER 4

SIX HOURS THAT CHANGED MY LIFE

WORDS OF PASSION FROM MATTHEW 27

MANY IMPORTANT DATES IN HISTORY HAVE been burned into the minds of Americans. They have altered circumstances and changed ideas, bringing extinction to some things while bringing new beginnings to others.

December 7, 1941.
November 22, 1963.
July 4, 1976.
September 11, 2001.

From the time North America was discovered, to the day the first automobile was sold, to the time the first rocket ship soared into space, significant events have transformed and shaped our lives. As great as these discoveries and inventions are, however, you have to go back further than 1492— before Columbus, before Galileo, before Copernicus, before Marco Polo, and before Constantine— to find the thing that changed my life.

It was not an era. It was not a span of months or days or years. It was but a breath, a moment in time, just six hours—that's all, just six hours. But what happened in those six precious hours has changed my life, my past, and my future forever!

I pray that it has changed your life, as well. Or if not, I pray it will change your life this Easter.

THE TIME BEFORE

My story begins early on a Friday morning around 33 A.D.—springtime in Jerusalem. On the Thursday night before, as Jesus had finished eating and instituting a new Passover meal with His disciples, He had shared some unexpected news with them. He said because of His love for them, because of His desire to redeem them from their sins and give them eternal life, He would be handed over to the local religious leaders, who in turn would hand Him over to the local Roman government and demand that He be killed immediately for sedition and blasphemy.

How could that be?

Yet later that same night, Jesus withdrew to the Garden of Gethsemane to pray to His Heavenly Father. He agonized about what lay ahead—not because He was fearful of physical death, but because the sinless One would become the sin offering for the sins of the world. His death would be *worse* than death, because it would carry the full weight of human sin. His human nature shrank from the thought of it—so

> **HE OFFERED PRAYERS AND APPEALS, WITH LOUD CRIES AND TEARS.**
> **(HEBREWS 5:7)**

deeply, in fact, that the Bible says He sweat great drops of blood.

What anguish! What agony! He would become the Passover Lamb, the sacrificial Lamb that would take away the sins of His people. There was no other way to redeem man, this crown of God's creation. From the moment Adam and Eve sinned in the Garden of Eden, God in His love sought to get Him back, salvaging man from sin, death, hell, and the grave. Jesus was the way.

Not long after Jesus' prayer in the Garden, one of His very own friends showed up with a posse to arrest Him. Yet He called Judas "friend" as He was being handed over to the religious leaders. They arrested Him on trumped-up charges by people who were threatened by Him, who were afraid of Him, who wanted to rid themselves of Him because of the convicting power of His words that rang in their heads. They truly despised and rejected Him.

Jesus, gentleman that He is, was almost silent. Only once did He answer their taunts and accusations—and even then, it wasn't out of retaliation or revenge but to inject truth into this situation, to fulfill His obedience to divine prophecy.

He was then handed over to Pontius Pilate—a man who even in his wicked, suspicious heart could find no reason to execute this carpenter's son from Nazareth. Still, because of public outrage by the religious establishment, he caved to their desires for Jesus to be killed.

But first—torture.

Jesus was beaten, bruised, whipped, struck. His beard was plucked out. His back was made raw by the infliction of the scourge straps. A crown of large thorns was forced down over His head. He was spit on, ridiculed, stripped, and mocked. This was just the beginning of the six hours that changed my life.

Can you imagine, after going through all of that, how He could still continue on, knowing that the worst was yet to come? But if He truly wanted to be our friend, it would cost Him more. More than the thorns, more than the beatings, more than the shame of it all, more than being stripped and made to walk naked in public with His back opened up by wounds, more than the laughing, more than the hissing and comments. It would cost Him more to be our friend.

THE HIGH PRICE OF FRIENDSHIP

Neither you nor I can be the friend of God without provision having been made for our sins. God's holiness requires that no sin enter His presence, and we are full of sin. Therefore, our salvation required a sinless substitute, a holy offering, a spotless sacrifice to die in our place. That sacrifice, that substitute, that offering, was Jesus Christ, God's only begotten Son.

He made the One who did not know sin to be sin for us, so that we might become the righteousness of God in Him."

2 Corinthians 5:21

What grace! What undeserved, illogical grace! God has not applied our sin to our account. Instead, He has "imputed" or attributed them to Jesus, though He is sinless in every respect. Jesus bore our sins on the Cross and endured the penalty we deserved that we might become the righteousness of God in Christ, for "without the shedding of blood there is no forgiveness" (Heb. 9:22).

THAT HE MIGHT NOW APPEAR IN THE PRESENCE OF GOD FOR US. (HEBREWS 9:24)

Because God loves us, He took everything about us that was bad and sinful, dirty and wrong, sick and diseased, and He charged His own Son with the penalty of it all. Jesus alone could pay the price. And because of that, Father God can take everything that Jesus was and is and attribute it to us when we receive His Son as our personal Lord and Savior.

He put my sin on Jesus, and Jesus' righteousness on me.
He put my troubled mind on Jesus, and Jesus' peace on me.
He put my sickness on Jesus, and Jesus' healing on me.
He put my fear on Jesus, and Jesus' boldness on me.
He put my dishonor on Jesus, and Jesus' honor on me.

God pulled a switch. He took Jesus spotless, sinless record and superimposed it over my life, washing away my sins by the blood of His dear Son.

THE LENGTHENING SHADOWS

The Bible tells us that by the time that Jesus had reached Golgotha, He had already needed help carrying His Cross because of His weakened condition. As He approached the place of crucifixion, with His arms attached to the horizontal Cross beam, He willingly lay down on the other. As they attached the beams together, they then attached Jesus to the Cross by nailing each of His hands, then His feet, to the wood. Roman tradition tells us that next they would have hoisted the Cross upwards with ropes until the base of the wood dropped into the hole that was dug to support it, causing it to stand upright. And there between two thieves Jesus was crucified to set us free—even the very ones who had enacted His execution. On a hillside in Jerusalem, the Good Shepherd willingly offered His life for ours.

And thus began six hours to purchase my pardon, six hours to purchase my freedom, six hours to free me from the prison I was in. Six hours to heal me of all of my sickness, to give me peace which the world can never take away, to wash my past away. Six hours in order to forgive me for everything I've ever done wrong, to secure my future with Him so we could be together forever.

DARKNESS COVERED THE LAND

From noon until three in the afternoon darkness came over the whole land. At about three in the afternoon Jesus cried out with a loud voice, "Elí, Elí, lemá sabachtháni?" that is, "My God, My God, why have You forsaken Me?"

Matthew 27:45–46

I wonder what must have gone through the minds of people who were nowhere near Golgotha that day. Maybe doing their laundry, cooking lunch, or preparing dinner. Then suddenly, the sky grew dark at midday, the elements of nature reacting in awe of the very One who spoke them into existence.

As He bled on the Cross, a soldier pierced His side with a spear, laying the flesh open. Jesus was pouring out His very life—literally—in order to save mine. And yours. He could not save Himself and still be the Savior of His people, His flock. He had to finish what He started. This was what He came to do, to "lay down his life for his friends" (John 15:13).

It wasn't the nails that held Him to the Cross. It wasn't the spear pierced in His side. It wasn't the crown of thorns upon His head. It was love that held Him there. Love—matchless, endless, unconditional, all-encompassing love. The world had never seen such a public display of affection before—and we never have since!

It all came down to six hours one Friday.

All the prophecies, all the promises, all the prophets, all the sacrifices, all the Scriptures, all the deliverances, all the healings, all the leading and guiding, all the kings, all the priests, even the Fall in the Garden of Eden—it all came down to six hours one Friday in Jerusalem when the relationship was restored between God and man.

Those six hours changed the world and altered history. Those six hours changed my life and gave me a future. Those six hours have given me hope and a promise. I am clean before the Lord of Glory because of those six hours.

ALONE

Heaven was silent during those six hours as friendship with God was purchased with the blood of the Savior. How the angels must have wanted desperately to step in and rescue their King and Creator. But Jesus was left alone to die. How vastly different this was from thirty-three years earlier when the host of heaven had filled the nighttime sky over Bethlehem announcing His birth with great joy.

Jesus was all by Himself when He purchased our salvation. No friends to comfort Him. No one to encourage Him. Even those nearby were trying to hide in the crowd to keep from being recognized as one of His friends. Jesus was called the friend of tax collectors and sinners. He never knew someone He didn't love. And yet now, like a stranger in His own land, it all came down to six lonely, agonizing, excruciating hours.

Don't you think it's silly by comparison when we talk about the "sacrifices" we've made for God? Isn't it ridiculous when we say we've "sacrificed" to be at

> **YOU HAVE RECEIVED FREE OF CHARGE; GIVE FREE OF CHARGE.**
> **(MATTHEW 10:8)**

church or to work in the ministry? How dare I ever say that I have given up anything to serve Jesus! We haven't learned anything about suffering. We have understood nothing of His pain. We rarely cry over the spiritual condition of those around us.

Those six hours He spent in agony make me want to serve and love Him more. They make me ashamed that I've done so little.

YOU ARE HIS JOY

Looking unto Jesus, the author and finisher of our faith, who for the joy that was set before Him endured the cross, *despising the shame, and has sat down at the right hand of the throne of God.*

Hebrews 12:2 (NKJV)

What was the "joy that was set before Him"? It was you! The one central issue that propelled Him forward, the one thing that would not let Him stop—was YOU! You were what drove Him. It was you that caused Him to finish what He started. It was you who came before His face when He thought He was going to pass out from the pain inflicted upon Him.

When He said in the Garden, "My Father, if this cannot pass unless I drink it, Your will be done" (Matt. 26:42), it was your name that filled His heart.

With every hammer strike on the nail, He was thinking about you. With every insult hurled in His face, He closed His eyes and thought of you. When the spear was thrust into His side and another wave of pain swept over Him, it was your face again coming before Him, motivating and pushing and convincing Him to go all the way.

You were the joy that the Father set before Him. The joy of knowing you throughout eternity. The joy of loving you completely. The joy of sharing in your existence. The joy of saving you and giving you life with Him forever. It was all for you!

It all came down to six hours one Friday. Those six hours changed my life. And those same six hours can change your life. Perhaps they already have. Jesus' last words as He was dying to redeem us were, "It is finished!" In the original language, this indicates that the work of redemption—of buying us back—had been accomplished and completed once and for all, and that its results are abiding continuously.

In other words, He finished it for everyone in every generation who hears and responds to His Gospel. Let it be finished in your life today. Oh, what a price He paid! How expensive it was to be our Friend.

BOUND ONLY ONCE
DAVID M. EDWARDS/MARGARET BECKER

Verse 1

Creation groaned, the earth did grieve
When God's own Son hung on a tree
Willingly His life for us
'Twas bound only once

Verse 2

Never could they hold Him down
No defeat for love's dear crown
Greater glory ne'er displayed
By the Author of this grace

Chorus 1

Bound only once to set me free
Tears and blood poured down for me
Precious Savior, Wounded Priest
'Twas bound only once
Bound only once

Verse 3

What Deity would leave His throne
To search the earth for only one
Gather up our filthy flesh
And crown it in His righteousness?

©2002 New Spring Publishing, Inc. / Nail Prince Music (ASCAP) Admin. by Brentwood-Benson Music Publishing, Inc. / Van Ness Press, Inc. (ASCAP) / Modern M Music (SESAC) Admin. by Music Services, Inc.

NAIL PRINCE
DAVID M. EDWARDS

Verse 1
It must have shocked the whole of heaven
When You left Your throne
The angels must have fallen silent
As You stepped out on Your own
When You came to love me
When You came to love me

Chorus
Deep wounds—my healing
Shed blood—my sin's remission
One cross—my forever
You must be the Nail Prince
You must be the Nail Prince
Jesus, You're the Nail Prince
Who loved me

Verse 2
I was a slave to isolation
Cut off from holy things
How I hungered for Your presence
Needing You to intervene
Then You came to love me
Then You came to love me

MEANT FOR KINGS
DAVID M. EDWARDS/MARGARET BECKER

Verse 1
Thirsty—
All our wells have run dry
Desperate on our knees
Now we cry
Fractured—
Our hearts lay in pieces
Mercy come bring
Healing to us

Chorus
You were pierced for all
That's gone unspoken
You were bruised
For now and yet to come
Scandalous—
This priceless holy treasure
Meant for kings
But lavished on the shunned

Verse 2
Hungry—
For Your touch in our lives
Thankful to find grace
In Your eyes
Blood brought
Peace beyond all measure
Purchased by our
Wounded Savior

Verse 3
How then—
How then do we praise You?
What can bear
The weight of response?
Nothing—
Nothing in or of us
For You know without You,
We're crushed

THANK YOU FOR THE CROSS

DAVID M. EDWARDS

Verse 1
Nowhere to run, nowhere to hide
Just a life adrift on the human tide
Had no sense of hope
I was dead inside
Until You took me in and You gave me life

Chorus
Thank You for the cross
Where You died for me
Thank You for the cross
Where love set me free
For it was Your blood
Flowing from Your head
Hands and feet
And Your bleeding side
Thank You for the cross, Jesus

Verse 2
What a mystery, You made a place for me
Somewhere safe and warm
A shelter from the storm
A precious sacrifice opened paradise
Forgiven of my sin, I now enter in

DAVID M. EDWARDS

David has been in ministry for fifteen years, and new songs of worship have been pouring out of him nearly all his life. He has worked with prolific songwriters such as Margaret Becker, Ginny Owens, Chris Eaton, Steve Hindalong, Greg Nelson, Natalie Grant, Matt Brouwer, Caleb Quaye, and John Hartley.

In 2003, he began his "Power to Worship Encounter," a popular seminar where attendees not only learn about the nuts and bolts of worship but experience God's presence as well. In 2005, he was awarded *Worship Leader* Magazine's "Best Scripture Song" Award for his song, "Create In Me," featured on his *Faithfully Yours: Psalms* project with Margaret Becker. Truly, this is only the beginning.

For more on David's music and ministry, contact: The Select Artist Group, P. O. Box 1418, LaVergne, Tennessee 37086, www.theselectartistgroup.com. Or visit www.davidmedwards.com.

Besides the three companion releases in the *Worship Through the Seasons* series, David's other books include a Psalms series—*Faithfully Yours*—as well as his signature work, *Worship 365*, and the *Holman CSB® Personal Worship Bible*, with more to come.

ACKNOWLEDGEMENTS

I wish to express my sincere appreciation to my publisher, David Shepherd, for being open to the things of God and open to me. To Ken Stephens, John Thompson, Jean Eckenrode, Jeff Godby, Lawrence Kimbrough, and the entire B&H family—my sincere thanks for all you've done for me.

To my literary agent, David Sanford, and the entire staff at Sanford Communications, Inc.—thank you so much for your guidance and perseverance. I would in particular like to thank my editor, Elizabeth Jones, for a phenomenal job and for working so quickly.

To my manager, Glenda J. McNalley, I wish to express my deep appreciation for her tireless efforts on my behalf and for her unwavering friendship.

To my beautiful wife, Susan, thank you for your love and standing by my side. *I love you!* To our wonderful blessings, Tara, Elyse, and Evan—Daddy loves you so much.

To my parents, Louis and Wanda Edwards, thank you for living out your "Passion" for the Lord. To my brother, Daniel, thank you for always being a faithful friend.

ALSO AVAILABLE FROM DAVID M. EDWARDS AND B&H PUBLISHING GROUP

FAITHFULLY YOURS:
WORSHIPFUL DEVOTIONS FROM THE PSALMS
EACH BOOK INCLUDES A 4 SONG WORSHIP CD
    CREATE IN ME ISBN: 0-8054-4329-0
    ENTER HIS GATES ISBN: 0-8054-4330-4
    AS HIGH AS THE HEAVENS ISBN: 0-8054-4331-2

WORSHIP 365 ISBN: 0-8054-4367-3
DAVID'S SIGNATURE WORK ON WORSHIP

THE PERSONAL WORSHIP BIBLE ISBN: 1-58640-280-3
FEATURING THE HOLMAN CHRISTIAN STANDARD BIBLE©

WORSHIP THROUGH THE SEASONS
    ADVENT: SEASON OF PROMISE ISBN: 0-8054-4324-X
    HARVEST: SEASON OF PROVISION ISBN: 0-8054-4333-9
    EASTER: SEASON OF PASSION ISBN: 0-8054-4332-0
    PENTECOST: SEASON OF POWER ISBN: 0-8054-4334-7

Available at bookstores and online retailers everywhere, or at BHPublishingGroup.com